The Tuskegee Airmen's
MISSION
to BERLIN

A FLY on the WALL HISTORY

BY THOMAS KINGSLEY TROUPE   ILLUSTRATED BY JOMIKE TEJIDO

PICTURE WINDOW BOOKS
a capstone imprint

Hi, I'm Maggie, and this is my brother, Horace.

We've been "flies on the wall" during important events in history.

We saw Pablo Picasso shock the world with his paintings.

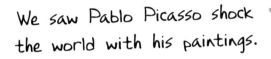

We even watched the Berlin Wall crumble to the ground!

We rode with settlers traveling west along the Oregon Trail.

One of our most dangerous adventures? It happened high in the sky toward the end of World War II (1939-1945) . . . .

Horace and I were flying around southern Italy in February 1944. A man named Adolf Hitler had risen to power in Germany. His followers were called Nazis. Under Hitler's command, the Nazis attacked many European and African countries and killed millions of people.

A large group of countries called the Allies fought against Hitler and his armies. Major members of the Allies included China, France, Great Britain, the Soviet Union, and the United States.

WORLD WAR II EUROPE
Allies   Axis Powers   Neutral

Germany

Italy

It's dangerous to be in Europe, Maggie.

Even for a fly!

I know.

It's not safe on land, on water, or in the air!

✶ ✶ ✶

The countries fighting alongside Germany were called the Axis powers. Germany's two main partners were Italy and Japan.

✶ ✶ ✶

We noticed a small airfield, and Horace got excited. He loves airplanes. We learned that the Allies had pushed the Germans out of the area. Ramitelli Airfield was now the home base for a group of U.S. fighter pilots. They were called the Tuskegee Airmen.

* * *

The Tuskegee Airmen were named after the airfield where they had trained. It was located in Tuskegee, Alabama. Ramitelli Airfield, in southern Italy, was the base for the 332nd Fighter Group.

* * *

The Tuskegee Airmen were African-American. This fact made them unusual. At the time, U.S. laws said that blacks couldn't eat, sleep, study, play, or work in many of the places whites did. Most pilots in the U.S. military were white. Few people believed blacks could fly a plane as well as whites.

What difference does a pilot's skin color make, Maggie? A good pilot is a good pilot!

I agree!

But some people can't see past a person's color.

These airmen were fighting a war AND fighting racism at the same time.

The soldiers met and slept in farmhouses near the edge of the airfield. We flew inside one of them to check it out. A group of pilots huddled around a table. They were listening to their leader, Colonel Benjamin O. Davis, Jr.

* * *

Colonel Davis was one of the first African-American pilots in the military. In 1954 he became the first black U.S. Air Force general.

* * *

"The whole world is watching us. You know that," the colonel told his men. "And the truth is, many folks expect us to fail. I want you to prove them wrong!"

It sounds like these pilots are under a lot of extra pressure to do well.

They are! But they've trained hard and know what they need to do.

I'm not worried.

Horace and I wanted to see the Tuskegee Airmen in action. So we snuck aboard an airplane with Colonel Davis during a practice run. The plane really took off! We were almost thrown back against the colonel's goggles!

Colonel Davis and his men flew over a train yard and began firing. Boxcars and engines exploded. BOOM! BOOM! BOOM! The airmen turned buildings into rubble.

Whoa!
They're really blowing stuff up!

These guys are amazing pilots. But I can't look!
They're flying SUPER close to the ground!
Yikes!

* * *

Most of the Tuskegee Airmen's missions included destroying enemy supplies. But the pilots were also asked to destroy bridges and communication centers.

* * *

Horace and I stuck around the Ramitelli Airfield for a few weeks. We watched the airmen practice and go on missions.

Then one day Colonel Davis had some big news. The Tuskegee Airmen would begin escorting heavy bombers into Germany. (I wasn't sure what that meant, but the pilots were very excited.)

10

More bombs?

Haven't they blown up enough stuff?

This time, I think they'll be flying alongside big airplanes that drop lots of bombs.

★ ★ ★

The Tuskegee Airmen were assigned to protect the 15th Air Force Heavy Bomber units. Heavy bombers such as B-17s and B-24s were among the largest planes in the military. Their bomb loads averaged 6,000 to 8,000 pounds (2,722–3,629 kilograms).

★ ★ ★

To help the men with their new missions, they received new airplanes from the U.S. military. Everyone seemed happy with the fighters. The P-51 Mustangs were fast and sleek. They were also able to fly long distances without refueling.

I'm confused. Mustangs are horses, not planes. I know horses, and they don't fly.

Well, horses don't fly, but these planes sure do. So maybe they're like horseflies?

* * *

There were many kinds of WWII fighter planes, including Mustangs, Warhawks, Bearcats, Corsairs, Kingcobras, and Thunderbolts.

* * *

Horace and I watched as the pilots tested out their new rides. They seemed faster than their older planes. The men thought this would help them defend the bombers while on their missions.

After a practice run one day, one of the pilots grabbed a brush and a can of red paint. He began painting the tail of his airplane. Other pilots did the same. I thought the silver fighters looked nice the way they were. But, whatever . . .

The nose cones of the planes are red too. Why aren't the men called the "Red Noses"?

I think it's because the tails are bigger and easier to see than the noses.

* * *

The bright-red paint helped pilots tell the difference between friends and foes in the air. In time, the Tuskegee Airmen were known as the "Red Tails" or "Red Tail Angels."

* * *

The Tuskegee Airmen flew a number of escort missions. They did really well. Soon bomber pilots asked if the "Red Tails" could escort them on their missions.

On the morning of March 24, a large group of airmen gathered. Colonel Davis told them about their biggest, most important mission yet. The Red Tails would escort B-17 bombers partway to Berlin, Germany. Then another fighter group would meet them and take the bombers the rest of the way.

Have you ever seen a B-17 bomber, Maggie? Those planes are huge!

The Red Tails are ready for the job, Horace.

I can't wait to watch them make history!

★ ★ ★

The B-17 bomber was called the *Flying Fortress* because of its giant size.

★ ★ ★

16

Horace and I buzzed aboard Captain Roscoe Brown's airplane. In a blink, we were in the sky, and the mission was underway.

The Red Tails flew close to the bombers. Everything seemed to be going well. But when we arrived at the "meet up" spot, the other fighter group wasn't there. It was late! Colonel Davis ordered his men to keep going. They would escort the B-17s all the way to Berlin.

As we neared the final target, trouble appeared. Enemy jets!

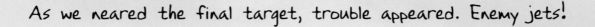

We've got company, Maggie!
German jets coming in!

Whoa! Look at those things move!

★ ★ ★

The Messerschmitt Me 262 was the world's first jet-powered fighter plane.
It could fly around 100 miles (160 kilometers) per hour *faster* than the P-51 Mustang.

★ ★ ★

The fast-flying German jets shot at the Red Tails. Colonel Davis' fighter had engine trouble, so he had to drop out of formation and return to the airfield. He ordered the Red Tails to stay with the bombers — no matter what.

Captain Armour G. McDaniel took over as the leader. But before we knew it, his plane was shot down. He ejected and parachuted behind enemy lines. Things didn't look good for the Red Tails or the mission! Or us!

Why aren't the Red Tails chasing those German planes?

If they leave the bombers, the Nazis will shoot the bombers down.

They're protecting them.

* * *

Captain McDaniel survived being shot down. He was captured by the enemy and later freed when the war ended.

* * *

21

We didn't have time to think, though. A German jet screamed past our plane. Captain Brown pulled up and fired his guns. *RATATAT!* The jet burst into flames. We got one! Shortly after, Lieutenant Charles Brantley fired — *RATATAT!* — and hit his mark too. A second enemy plane down!

The bomber group was getting very close to its target. First Lieutenant Earl Lane aimed his sights at another jet. He fired. RATATAT! The jet began to smoke, and a piece flew off. A total of three German planes were down!

They knocked three super-fast jets out of the sky!

That's amazing!

I don't know how the Red Tails did it.

And the big target is still coming up!

* * *

The Nazis called their new technology *Wunderwaffe*. The term is a German word that means "wonder weapon."

* * *

23

In no time, the B-17s were flying over their target. Horace and
I watched as giant bombs dropped from their bellies.

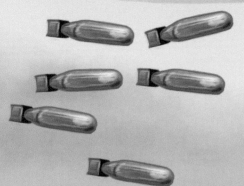

The target was a tank factory the Nazis were using to build more
weapons. The bombs struck, and the building exploded. BOOM! BOOM!
BOOM! The B-17s had hit their mark!

The Daimler-Benz plant was more than 70 percent destroyed because of the Red Tails' escort mission.
Though the mission was a success, two of the B-17 bombers were shot down.

★ ★ ★

Once we were all back at the base, the Tuskegee Airmen celebrated. They'd completed the longest bomber escort mission in World War II. Colonel Davis was proud of his pilots.

* * *

The Red Tails' escort mission to Berlin was 1,600 miles (2,575 km) round trip.

* * *

The Red Tails earned many awards for their incredible service. They did so well, they were given the Presidential Unit Citation. They proved, once and for all, that African-American pilots belonged in the air too.

I said it! Good pilots are good pilots, no matter what color their skin is.

These men are going to be legends, Horace.

Everyone will remember how the Tuskegee Airmen helped the Allies win the war.

On May 7, 1945, Germany surrendered to the Allies. Three months later Japan also surrendered. World War II was over! Soldiers were free to return to their homes and families.

The Tuskegee Airmen proved to the world that they belonged in the air. Their efforts helped the U.S. military work toward equal treatment of all soldiers.

TIMELINE

MAY 1939
U.S. Senator Harry S. Truman helps put forth a bill to allow black pilots to serve in the Civilian Pilot Training Program.

JANUARY 16, 1941
The 99th Pursuit Squadron is formed and will begin training at Tuskegee Army Air Field in Tuskegee, Alabama, in July.

DECEMBER 1940
The U.S. Army Air Corps decides to "experiment" by forming an all-black fighter squadron with 33 pilots.

MARCH 7, 1942
The first class of Tuskegee Airmen graduates from training.

SEPTEMBER 10, 1944
Four pilots of the 332nd Fighter Group receive Distinguished Flying Cross medals.

JULY 2, 1943
Captain Charles B. Hall is the first Tuskegee Airman to shoot down an enemy airplane.

JUNE 25, 1944
Pilots of the 302nd Fighter Squadron seriously damage a German destroyer.

MARCH 24, 1945
The Tuskegee Airmen complete their mission to Berlin, Germany – the longest bomber escort mission in World War II. They shoot down three enemy fighters along the way.

AUGUST 14, 1945
World War II ends with the surrender of Japan.

JULY 26, 1948
President Harry S. Truman signs Executive Order 9981. It declares that all people in the U.S. Armed Forces should be treated equally, regardless of race.

GLOSSARY

Allies–the group of countries united against Germany during World War II, including China, France, Great Britain, the Soviet Union, the United States, and others

Axis powers–the group of countries united against the Allies during World War II, including Germany, Italy, and Japan

eject–to force one's way out

escort–to travel with and protect

formation–a group of airplanes flying together in a pattern

mission–a military task

Nazi–a member of a political party led by Adolf Hitler; the Nazis ruled Germany from 1933 to 1945

racism–the belief that one race is better than another race

sleek–smooth and shiny

squadron–a unit of the military

surrender–to give up or stop fighting a battle

World War II–war from 1939 to 1945 between the Allies and the Axis powers; the Allies won

THINK ABOUT IT

1. Colonel Davis told his men, "The whole world is watching us. You know that. And the truth is, many folks expect us to fail." Why were they expected to fail, and how did the Tuskegee Airmen prove themselves?

2. Describe what's happening in the illustration on pages 18 and 19. Talk about the planes you see – which side are they fighting for, what are they doing, where are they going, and what's going to happen to them next?

READ MORE

Kuenstler, Mort, and James I. Roberston, Jr. *World War II: 1939-1945.* See American History. New York: Abbeville Press Publishers, 2016.

Summers, Elizabeth. *Weapons and Vehicles of World War II.* Tools of War. North Mankato, Minn.: Capstone Press, 2016.

Thompson, Ben. *World War II.* Guts & Glory. New York; Boston: Little, Brown and Company, 2016.

INTERNET SITES

Use FactHound to find Internet sites related to this book:

Visit *www.facthound.com*

Just type in 9781515816003 and go.

Check out projects, games and lots more at
www.capstonekids.com

INDEX

Look for other books in the series:

Special thanks to our adviser, Kevin Byrne, PhD, Professor Emeritus of History, Gustavus Adolphus College, for his expertise.

Picture Window Books is published by Capstone,
1710 Roe Crest Drive, North Mankato, Minnesota 56003
www.mycapstone.com

Library of Congress Cataloging-in-Publication data is available on the Library of Congress website.
ISBN 978-1-5158-1600-3 (library binding)
ISBN 978-1-5158-1604-1 (paperback)
ISBN 978-1-5158-1608-9 (eBook PDF)

Summary: Describes the events leading up to and including the Tuskegee Airmen's historic B17 bomber-escort mission to Berlin, Germany, during World War II.

Editor: Jill Kalz
Designer: Sarah Bennett
Creative Director: Nathan Gassman
Production Specialist: Laura Manthe

The illustrations in this book were planned with pencil on paper and finished with digital paints.

Printed and bound in the United States of America.
010850S18